EMBRACING STRENGTH & PURPOSE IN THE MIDST OF YOUR STORM

Encouraging Words During a Difficult Season

REVEREND MICHAEL GAMBLE

WESTBOW
PRESS®
A DIVISION OF THOMAS NELSON
& ZONDERVAN

WestBow Press books may be ordered through booksellers or by contacting:

WestBow Press
A Division of Thomas Nelson & Zondervan
1663 Liberty Drive
Bloomington, IN 47403
www.westbowpress.com
844-714-3454

Scripture quotations marked KJV are taken from the King James Version.

Scripture quotations marked NIV are taken from The Holy Bible, New International Version®, NIV® Copyright © 1973, 1978, 1984, 2011 by Biblica, Inc.® Used by permission. All rights reserved worldwide.

ISBN: 978-1-6642-3708-7 (sc)
ISBN: 978-1-6642-3709-4 (e)

Print information available on the last page.

WestBow Press rev. date: 06/23/2021

In Loving Memory of My Grandparents

Henry and Coreen Gamble
Addie and Clifton Tindal

A Salute to a Falling Soldier and Friend
PFC MichaelAngelo Mora

Contents

Introduction

The best time to spend during the day or night is time with God. It doesn't matter what kind of a chaotic or busy day you are having, you would be astonished at the difference your day would be spending it with God. Over the years, God had given me the ability to trust his word so much that it has always been a reliable source for me. Now, in that powerful storm when everything seemed undetermined, I had to make a choice: would I trust my sensitivities or God's Word?

The world we live in seems to have so much confusion and dark clouds that it shows evidence of erupting storms of despair and hardships. The distractions of social and news media, and the entertainment world have disturbed our souls so much that we have allowed it to drown out the voice of God. It is not that God isn't speaking loud or abrasive, it is because we have not calmed our souls enough to hear him.

Although you and I follow our God-given aspirations we will encounter numerous storms. Some will be moderate; others will be challenging. The life that we live on this earth is full of difficulties. When we can go to church, God will occasionally speak to us through the message, through a song, through someone in the service or God may speak clearly to us when we come in and begin to seek His face and will. One important thing, we must consider praying and seeking God.

The message in this book, "Embracing Strength & Purpose In the Midst of Your Storm" is designed for you to take the time to form a relationship with God, study his word, and reflect on his goodness which will enhance your life in incredible ways.

We will encounter storms and question our purpose at times therefore I pray that this spiritual message will be a breaking point in your life to carve spending time with God making him a priority in your life while finding your strength, purpose, and shelter from your storm. Remember this, you are destined for a breakthrough.

Dedications and Thanks

I dedicate this book to my best friend, my ride or die my coach, and my #1 motivator, my wife Rev Shirley J. Gamble. Thank you, Shirley, for loving me. You know that God is the only one that loves you more than I do.

To my Two children Johnathon, Gabriel, and son-in-law Martiece to whom I am proud. To my precious grandbaby Zhuri thank you for loving your Granddad (G-daddy). I love you all very much.

To my mother and father, Ella, and Otis Gamble. Sister and brother, Martrell Matthews, and Marland Gamble, my Aunts Rosa Lee Tindal and Dorothy Mae Davis. To all my in-laws, thank you for your support and inspiration in all that I do. And to every church member from Morning Star Missionary Baptist Church and my Pastor Harold H. Craig Jr., you all encouraged me, motivated me, and loved me through every step. You have inspired me in ways you may never know. I Thank You.

To My battle buddies in the Army, it has been a journey, we trained, prayed and fought in the wars together and we made it home, Thank you for the memories!

Chapter 1

Your Purpose, Your Calling

God's Purpose for your life is that you would
sculpture your life around his image.

Your Calling and your purpose are not the same. Your Calling is the distinctive path God has for you that leads you towards the last destination which your purpose. Your purpose is to prepare your life and sculpt it around the image and glory of God and show that image and glory to the world. Your calling comes from within you, but the focus is not on you but God.

We all were created with a purpose to worship and glorify God. This means the way we live makes those around us want to know God and be intrigued with God. Our joy, light, and glory makes our co-workers, neighbors, and friends be attracted to him, and therefore we exist. We fulfill our purpose by living out our calling whatever it may be. What is your purpose? My purpose is to make God known to others and to elevate him. Our Calling is how God uses us to achieve his work. God's Plan has been established for your success in which your purpose follows. Therefore, be delighted that you have a greater purpose in life, for this implies that your life is momentous and not hectic.

We are all valuable pieces of a puzzle. We are shaped differently and fit in unique places, but we have the same purpose. When God puts us together and unravels the puzzle, he is exalted. Because we are called by

God, we are in the household of God. We are God's ambassadors called to deliver a message, the word of God. It doesn't matter how you deliver the word of God, whether through song, dance, or poem as long as it is of God for the people of God.

Many people seek to find their purpose in life. They ask the question, "What is God's purpose for me"? What is my calling? The Spirit of God will lead and guide us. All we must do is respond. It is when we try to get ahead of the Spirit of God, we falter and fail. So, when the spirit moves in you, it will assist you in your purpose and your calling. A good place to start your journey would be to begin in prayer, read the bible, and seek guidance from your church leadership.

I recall while serving in the military, new in the area my wife and I started attending church one Sunday out of nowhere the pastor of this church ask us to sing, just get up and sing something. Although we sing around the house together, we never thought of singing in front of people. Well, after looking at each other for a second or two we got up, told the musician the song we would like to sing, and we blessed the congregation and our pastor. It went well and every week we were on the program to sing, which meant we had to learn a song every week before Sunday service. Our Pastor saw something in us. From that day, we found our calling and was able to fill in when needed to sing songs together in a church service or at any church I would be stationed. Today, during my retirement from the military and my wife from the Postal Service we are still singing together which lead us to receive our license to preach and publish books.

(Romans 8:14 KJV), " For as many as are led by the Spirit of God, they are the sons of God."

One of God's greatest gifts offered is the privilege of being led by the Spirit. The Holy Spirit has provided us wisdom to make good decisions. The ability to plug into our calling is much simpler when we make good decisions based on the leading and guiding of the Holy Spirit. Let us not forget that the Holy Spirit is powerful, it helps us during our weakest hour.

When we do not know what to pray for, the Holy Spirit intervenes for us through silent groans. Have you experienced the Holy Spirit? Is it a question in your mind? If it is? You will know the feeling. I have experienced the Holy Spirit moving in my life multiple times, it was so strong that it saved my life. Every person has been given gifts and talents wherever they may be. Spend a few moments thinking about your calling. It may or may not be in the center of your life, but your calling should not be placed on the back burner; it's merely your heart speaking its truth that you have been called, listen to it.

If you find yourself sitting on the edge of your bed, on your job, or in your car wondering if you have something to offer your church, make the choice, do inventory on your calling because you have a purpose to do his will. That is why God's Plan is created so that your calling will begin when you are prepared. What could be more dreadful for you than to recognize your calling and not be able to accomplish it? Think about this, to find your calling, ask yourself, "How are you bringing love, honor, praise, and worship to God and the world?" A person's calling is as distinctive as their fingerprint. Each person is shaped or constructed according to his or her calling. God was glorified by Jesus developing and accomplishing his calling on earth. We also glorify God by doing what God created us to do.

(Ephesians 4:1 KJV)… I therefore, the prisoner of the Lord, beseech you that ye walk worthy of the vocation wherewith ye are called, that is, to live a life that exhibits godly character, moral courage, personal integrity, and mature behavior a life that expresses gratitude to God for your salvation.

You may not think you have a purpose or calling to glorify God, but you do. There is someone either in your neighborhood, church, job, grocery store, or distant family member is waiting for you to use your calling, to help them get closer to God.

"Even every one that is called by my name: for I have created him for my glory, I have formed him; yea, I have made him". (Isaiah 43:7 KJV).

Our faithfulness can from time to time be determined by examining our priorities, or how we devote our time. When we are faithful to the callings God has placed upon our lives, we will experience implication, significance, and fullness. If our priorities are misaligned, we will not.

God, in his definitive project, places us in several seasons of life. I know that throughout my young life, I have been addicted to drugs and alcohol, enlisted, and retired from the Army and became a minister. Each place and each season are ordained by God. While it is okay to set goals and plans, instead of worrying about tomorrow, remember that God has you in mind and just where he would like you in this season of life. I used to let people convince me that I could not do something that I was passionate about. People can tell you whatever they want, but the truth is, the one and only person in charge of determining your destiny is God. What someone else say to you does not matter. If God gives you the idea, do it! I've found this to be so helpful in my own life. At the end of the day surround yourself with people that inspire you to be a better you spiritually. Remove people with negativity in your life and replace it with people who believe in you and want you to achieve your dreams to be "successful".

God can take you from a dark place in your life, help you find your purpose, and support you in achieving it because he sees something in you that will bless someone with your gift. Just remember you have come into the world with a purpose, when used probably it will develop and emerge spiritually. You must have a purpose in life because the purpose is life. It means that you have a destiny beyond this world. Just remember you have a purpose; you have a calling to make God and yourself proud let's go to the next chapter.

Chapter 2

God Removed Toxic Relationships from your Life for a Reason

Relationships and friendships can be toxic and considered bad storms. God gives us the strength to persevere, overcome and eliminate those storms in our lives to make us stronger from future challenges that may try to break us and eventually bring us down. If there is one thing I've learned to accept, is that not all people who look good on the outside are good on the inside. Not all people whom God put in your life will be there forever. So, don't worry about people God removed from your life, He heard conversations you didn't, saw things you couldn't, and made moves you wouldn't. If someone makes you become a better person, instead of a bitter person continue to unite with them. If not, let them go. Practice this statement "I have my values and principles if you don't agree with it, it's ok you can move on."

Don't be weary or shocked when your neighbors, family members, co-workers, or close friends disappoint you or let you down, God knows and heard your cry and He's answering your prayers. Don't be shocked if God removes each person that surrounds you as you pray for renewal. That also means God is now showing you the signs that you've been asking for and the solutions you need. Therefore, don't be surprised that God gives you the wake-up call you need even if you're not prepared or ready for it. You see, God filters our lives and removes the wrong people, and moves us in the right direction. He gives you simplicity when you have questions. The fact is, the more you ask for answers or for healing from God the more your life will change.

There are people in our lives that are leading us nowhere but down and somehow we agree to keep being led by them to a place where we know we do not want to go. I ask the question, are we dedicated? Are they supposed to be true friends or family members? Is loyalty a question? This affects our relationships, friendships, and in some cases partnerships. Sometimes, we don't dare to say no. At times, we're afraid we might hurt the person's feelings. Sometimes, we feel as if we have no choice. What we must understand is that what is not good for us, is not for us. Bottom line think about the reason they left before you run after them. If God has pressed His way in and removed the person from your life, take a second to breathe and thank Him. It might hurt now, but the pain will diminish with time.

I would like to make this clear. God's definitive plan is that we live eternally with him in his kingdom. When we give our lives to God, we are authorizing him to do his will in our lives. Consequently, anything or anyone that comes in the way of fulfilling God's plan in your life will be removed. Let's look at the following structures.

(1 Samuel 16:7 KJV) But the LORD said unto Samuel, look, not on his countenance, or on the height of his stature; because I have refused him: for the LORD seeth not as man seeth; for man looketh on the outward appearance, but the LORD looketh on the heart.

(Proverbs 25:5 KJV) Take away the wicked from before the king, and his throne shall be established in righteousness.

(1 Corinthians 5:13 KJV) But them that are without God judgeth. Therefore, put away from among yourselves that wicked person.

(Isaiah 57:14 KJV) And shall say, cast ye up, cast ye up, prepare the way, take up the stumbling block out of the way of my people."

This may be hard to realize but there may not be anything wrong or upsetting with your friendships or relationships, but God may remove someone from your life because they may be needed in a different place. At a moment's notice, God may call them to assist someone or something in need or call them home to be with him. Don't be weary because, (Romans 8:28 KJV) says "And we know that all things work together for good to those who love God, to those who are the called according to His purpose".

God removed several friendships from me throughout the years and when I look back, it was the best thing that could ever happen to me. I couldn't understand why but I later realized God knew it was for my good and that they weren't going to be my problem any longer, but burdens for God to bear. He was protecting me. He handled it, eventually, we were unfriended for whatever reasons and time to move on. The day I raised my hand and enlisted in the Army, I left all my drinking buddies, party brothers, and drug-using associates behind. A few of my old friends have passed away, some live hundreds of miles away and several I just don't know but I wish them well.

As a last resort cutting people out of your life is completely acceptable. I say this without reluctance since we're all so quick to find reasons to give up on one another (myself included), there's no reason why someone should stay in a place of abuse, endangerment, or spiritual downgrade. We must distinguish the difference between finding someone unpleasant and running from someone oppressively cruel.

God is always at work. We may not understand why God does the things he does but eventually, it will come to pass. We often fail to know God's unspoken guidance or protection as incidents in our lives unfold. But, when we look back at past experiences, we can see His hands cover our issues even in times of tragedy.

I recall when I was seventeen, I was involved in aggressive crimes that include theft, fights, drugs, gambling, women. I could not go anywhere without looking over my shoulders or looking in the rearview mirror contently. Things got worse, I receive a wake-up call when five of my homeboys were caught and are now serving life in prison and two of my close friends were killed. I had to separate myself from that madness, things had to change, I needed support. I was reminded of the scripture, (Psalms 121:1-3 KJV) I will lift up mine eyes unto the hills, from whence cometh my help. My help cometh from the LORD, which made heaven and earth. He will not suffer thy foot to be moved: he that keepeth thee will not slumber.

It was God's grace at work that enabled me to take control of my life. From the moment I stepped into my new life, God's favor began working nonstop on my behalf. Being born again was just the starting place for His favor to pour out. Therefore, I dedicated my life to Him as a "living sacrifice". There will always be speed bumps in your life, continue to walk in obedience to God and never doubt His power to get you through.

Chapter 3

Guarding Your Mind Against Satan

Your mind is a gift from God. It can store trillions of thoughts. And it is a tool that God wants to use in your ministry to achieve his purposes. To guard our mind, we must acknowledge ungodly thoughts and ideas by testing them against God's word. (Psalm 19:7 KJV) The law of the LORD is perfect, converting the soul: the testimony of the LORD is sure, making wise the simple. The statues of the LORD are trustworthy, making wise the simple. Have you ever thought that you may have lost your mind? Or thought it was out of control? With all the medications in the world of medicine, doctors have prescribed mind-altering remedies to help us gain control of what could be devastating if Satan gains control.

Our mind which could be led to a different understanding when exposed to the word of God can be so relaxed that it allows Satan to have his way. "So, I pledge to you" We must not let Satan take over.

(2 Corinthians 10:4-5 KJV) For the weapons of our warfare are not carnal, but mighty through God to the pulling down of strong holds; Casting down imaginations, and every high thing that exalteth itself against the knowledge of God and bringing into captivity every thought to the obedience of Christ.

Satan's objective is to target the mind, it is our major battlefield. He attacks every believer's mind with sexual images, evil and dangerous ungodly thoughts. He does this through the world structure which he rules his multitudes of demons. Satan recognizes that if he can control the mind, he can regulate the body. Satan's attack on our mind violates and assaults our eyes and ears. It is with our eyes and ears that we absorb obedience to God into the mind. Therefore, guard them with your whole heart and the word of God!

Satan is on a continuous campaign to destroy our lives by mixing toxic lies, impulses, and allegations into our everyday thoughts. When we are not surrounded by God's word, we start to doubt God's faithfulness. We begin to feel unproductive, anxious, and enticed to turn to worldly comforts. Destructive thoughts can circle so strongly in our minds that they start to lead our lives negatively. Every Christian should set up a "high-level security firewall" around each one of our thoughts one that forcefully removes the world's lies and acknowledges God's truths. Only in this way can we "secure" all our thoughts to make them obedient to Christ.

I remember a time in my life when I was not in control of my mind, drugs were. I allowed negative thoughts to saturate my thinking that almost cause me to lose my life. People kill themselves because of negative thoughts that somehow get into their minds. Bottom line, Satan does not care about us, he wants to rule our lives and he prefers that we disappear from God's sight so that he can destroy us. "Be sober, be vigilant; because your adversary the devil, as a roaring lion, walketh about, seeking whom he may devour" (1 Peter 5:8 KIV).

I do not know exactly how Satan might try to harm you; he can be highly intelligent and perform all types of ways to attack you. But as an overall principle, Satan always tries to find out where we are vulnerable, and then he will focus his attack on that area of our lives. For example, you have a problem with laziness or a lack of restraint, you can be certain that Satan will attempt to take advantage of that vulnerability.

The ability to think is God's vital gift to us; it sets man separately from the animals and locates him in the class of God. Thinking is one of the reasons man was created in the image of God. The Bible confirms the truth that man is a spirit, has a soul, and exists in a body. God effortlessly combines these components to create you for his glory. Our Thinking processes should take place where the spirit, soul, and body intersect. A question was asked, "How can you remain strong, even when Satan tries to turn you away from Christ?" One way is to stay close to God no matter what. The Bible reiterates "Resist the devil, and he will flee from you, Come near to God and he will come near to you" (James 4:7-8 NIV). I strongly believe that if you fill your mind of God, you will resist the devil's temptation. "Put on the full armor of God so that you can take your stand against the devil's schemes" (Ephesians 6:11 NIV). We cannot conquer Satan on our own but with God's help, we can.

Satan and his demons have no authority to create. They are limited to betraying us and destroying what God has created. The battle is in our minds. Satan will do all that he can to pull you away from your relationship with God and your victory. This battle is real and is the reason why so many Christians today live-in defeat and need the joy and peace God expected for them. Satan has been attacking our mind from the beginning and he will not be changing anytime soon.

But Satan's strategies are not new, he is always attempting to destroy us, so we need to be able to identify them. From the very first time he arrived on the scene he started deceiving Eve. He caused her to doubt God's word. He can make you imagine things that are not true or that never took place. Satan causes mayhem and makes you question just about anything. Satan is a fraud. Satan will try to deceive your mind into believing in him instead of what God says in his Word. Let's not give Satan the credit, you are wiser than that, God is much bigger than that. It's time for the next chapter.

Chapter 4

God Will See You Through It

You wake up praying for a day without controversy, defeat, or heartache. You are tired of hearing bad news and unsolvable matters. I remember spending long days and nights wondering how I am going to get through cancer. My diagnosis took me by surprise. There were days when I remember praying for strength to get through the next five minutes, the hour, or the week. I realized I was facing a difficult time in my life and needed help coping.

I have read testimonies of other men to include my father who was diagnosed in 2010, but never thought I would get prostate cancer. My option depended on several key factors to include the stage of prostate cancer. I chose Robotic Salvage Prostatectomy. If I ever needed God, it would be during my situation. I can say, the weeks of recovery were a little uncomfortable, but the doctors were great and the doctor in charge "GOD" I cannot express how great he was and is to me and how blessed I am because "HE SAW ME THROUGH" one of my darkest moments. He has always supplied plenty of what I need when I needed it. Not a moment too soon, and never a second late. We serve a mighty God.

You will endure a crisis during your life if you have not already, or if you are not in the middle of one right now, your time will come. God's people have identified "times of difficulty" and "days of sorrow" for thousands of years, and the same continues today. God never promised that we will not have problems in our lifetime. It is not about having trials and tribulations; it is how you get through them. God hears our cries for help, and they have or will be answered. This is who our God has been from the beginning, God of Abraham, and Isaac, this is whom Jacob through his ups and downs found God to be. The Scripture states: "God who answers me in the day of distress" (Genesis 35:3 KIV).

You have just been diagnosed with a serious illness. Your home is like a combat zone. You lost your job. You are failing several classes. Your church is in serious channels. The world is in distress with COVID-19. In seasons like this, many of us feel like we need something new. How do we weather seasons in life when everything we need has been stripped away? A word from God that pertains directly to our situation is a good start. We must trust that "God got this"! So, let's get to work on focusing on God.

Let us pray this out!!! God, please help me through this, assist me in keeping my eyes and ears concentrated on you instead of the situations around me. Speak serenity into my mind, calm my spirit, and rebuild my heart. Give me an insight into your purpose for me today. Quietly lead me out of this quarry. I am bruised and I need your help. Please open my eyes and heart to a blessing. Let your strength put a sparkle on me during this dark time in my life. Help me to be your hands and feet even when I feel damaged and feeble. I know you will be my strength, Amen.

Whatever you are going through, God promises that he will see you through and give you the power and focus you need. Rest assured; you are not on your own. God has not abandoned you and he has not singled you out, no matter how you feel. God wants you to know that he understands, how you feel, he knows more about your situation than you do, and that he saw it coming before you did.

I recall after I retired from Army stationed at Fort Hood, Texas I moved back to Kentucky, my wife who recently retired from the Postal Service and I would get up in the mornings eat breakfast, pray for change and head to the library, and research for jobs, this was every day 9 am until 3 pm. We applied to over 30 jobs a day. Why? Now that we have retired from a job working over 20 years, it was time for a change. It was stressful, our savings were going fast, we have two kids in high school and bills do not wait. We were spending days and nights trying to figure out our finances trying to adjust to the economy and retirement pay which was barely enough and regrouping into a world without the military's extra incentives, we needed a job and quick.

One day after a couple of hours at the library we were on the way home, I was so upset about not getting called for an interview, I kept going on and on about needing a job and questioning God's work. When I pulled into our driveway, I received a call for an interview, I could not believe it. I felt bad about not having patience and trusting God's timing. I went on the interview and nailed the job, 2 weeks later my wife was hired. God saw the need; His timing was impeccable which is not unusual.

Hardship is not only a bridge to a deeper relationship with God, but it is also the direction to independence, restoration, and maximum efficiency. The Lord uses trials as his precise tool, making careful and skillful incisions into your life that are insufferable at times, but also essential for you to be free of hidden issues that seek to weaken and ruin you.

Our God is too incredible to work according to our convenient timetables. He loves us too much to do just what we want when we want in our times of catastrophe. But he is there for us. He is aware of our predicament. And in Christ, he will respond, not when we want, but with the answer, we need for our victory and his glory. Some excellent news, isn't it? Let us move on to the next chapter and continue to claim our victory.

Chapter 5

His Grace is Sufficient

Grace is needed by everyone, from the prodigal son to the well-balanced righteous person who even now falls short and can simply look to God's grace for salvation. We can't save ourselves. Therefore, I will boast even more gladly about my weaknesses, so that Christ's power may rest on me.

Grace is found more than 150 times in the New Testament what a remarkable word and what it means to Christians today.

(2 Corinthians 12:9 KIV) reads, but he said to me, my grace is sufficient for you, for my power is made perfect in weakness.

(John 1:17 KIV) states that Grace is a continuous theme in the Bible, and it concludes in the New Testament with the coming of Jesus.

We serve a magnificently kind and compassionate God. He is a God who loves us deeply. He is always there when we need him. When we do not think we need him, he still is supplying and keeping us. Some of us do not give him credit. He is a compassionate provider and a gracious giver of all good things. There was a time in my life, while in my early twenties, I was so insecure, stressed, and disturb with the way my life was going. I was straight out of high school, to recover from the anxiety, I bought a car, bought nice clothes but was still living at home with my parents acting as though I had a big bank account. I was trying to impress my friends and buy friendships. But God's Grace taught me that it is not about me, it is about him, and that he purchased our freedom with the blood of his Son.

God's grace helped me to see that I was going down the wrong path. The journey to get here today was long and undignified, weird yet dangerous. Drugs and alcohol destroyed my relationship with family members, friendships, and opportunities. During the 1980's it was marijuana, cocaine and crack season being sold everywhere and people were being killed or overdosing from it. It started as a recreational thing for me then it became out of control. At the time I did not realize my life could get out of hand so quickly, but it did. But then there was God who had an incredible plan for me.

With his incredible love, I was able to take control of my destiny and know where I was going in my life. Has God helped you see your journey? There were times I would tell my kids to stay on the right path do not turn left or right, go straight, and continue to follow the cross. God wants you to listen to him and receive his word. If you want to be successful and seasoned in your spirituality trust in the lord. As Christians, we have the opportunity throughout the year to give thanks for what God has done in our lives. We can celebrate, anniversaries, birthdays, graduations, and births, there is always a time to rejoice in the Lord and thank him for his grace. So, let's celebrate him.

What I know about God is that he doesn't change. The year 2020 has been a trial year for our country but for those of us who are still standing, God has bought us through. You are surviving the conflict of the universe, COVID-19 in which we are facing. We cannot deny that our nation has issues, we turn on the television there is violence, fear, hatred, and corruption. I can say God is bringing you through an experience because he is faithful and is the same God he has always been, passionate, holy and his Grace is sufficient. "I am not ashamed of the gospel, because it is the power of God for salvation to everyone who believes" (Romans 1:16 KIV).

Grace is the free and unjust favor from God to Christians as created in the salvation of sinners and the granting of blessings. The teaching of the gospel is that grace is unjustified mercy that God gave to people by sending his Son, Jesus Christ, to die on a cross, hence securing man's eternal salvation from sin.

(Exodus 34:6-7 KIV), and he passed in front of Moses, proclaiming, "The LORD, the compassionate and gracious God, slow to anger, abounding in love and faithfulness, maintaining love to thousands, and forgiving wickedness, rebellion, and sin. Yet he does not leave the guilty unpunished; he punishes the children and their children for the sin of the parents to the third and fourth generation." "For by grace are you saved, through faith, and that not of yourselves" (Ephesians 2:8 KJV). These scriptures describe the peace and mission of grace. I am reminded, the Apostle Paul began many of his letters with the phrase, "Grace and peace to you from God our Father and the Lord Jesus Christ".

Have you ever confronted a situation, stressed about it all night, cried about it, and later God has been there, blessed you, and provided an answer for your situation by morning? One morning I got into my car started it, and it began to smoke. I did not know what to think, I knew that I did not have the money in my budget for a new engine or new car which would have been a couple of thousands of dollars. So, I prayed, I went to my mechanic, he looked over my car and found that I had an oil leak which could be repaired. Well, I can tell you how happy I became knowing that God was there and provided for me. It was just that simple.

God knows who you are and what you would be going through in your lifetime, he is there for you in your situation. I wonder what we will see God do for us tomorrow, next week, next month, or next year. We may face the enemy who will seek to destroy us. God is gracious and will take care of us. His Grace is sufficient. Countless people are giving up on the Church because they are tired of feeling like they are being let down, falling short. They have tried over and over, but they constantly feel like they are just not good enough. They don't understand grace.

Grace is not a turbocharge in a car that kicks up speed as needed. Instead, it is our constant energy source. It is not the light at the end of the tunnel but the light that pushes us through the tunnel. Grace is not accomplished somewhere down the road. It is accepted right here and right now. The grace of Christ is sufficient to cover our debt and sufficient to transform us. (Luke 1:37 KIV) says Grace is the presence of God's power. Grace is sufficient. It is enough. Don't quit. Keep striving. Don't look for an escape route and justifications. Look for the Lord and His great strength. Don't seek someone to condemn. Seek God, you will feel the supporting power and divine help we call His Amazing Grace.

We serve a God who turns our weakness into great strength. In his grace, all he asks of us is to have an open heart to receive him. He's the

God of kindness who heals the sick and spends time with the sinners rather than the religious. Our God lays down his life that we might live through him. So, go get your favorite cup of tea, coffee, or juice and continue to read the next chapter.

Chapter 6

Living with Your Faith and Belief

Faith is trust, guarantee, and confidence in God. Living faith is shown by service and obedience to God. The phrase "just have faith, it will work out" is used by people to encourage and reassure someone facing serious challenges or traumatic situations. Faith is the substance or assurance of things we hope for but have not yet received. Faith (confidence, belief, trust) is also our evidence of that which is not seen the invisible spiritual things. Faith comes before a prayer is answered or before a person has received what he or she has asked for from God.

Let us cover the difference between belief and faith. Belief is a strongly held view or a solid trust whereas faith is a strong religious belief. Belief is based on possibility or chance whereas faith is not based on possibility at all. Belief depends on proof whereas Faith is not. Belief is focused on faith whereas Faith is focused on trust. Faith and belief are parallel in ways. Yet, the New Testament does acknowledge that people can have untrue faith or lacking belief, which is ineffective. The difference is not between the two words but between the concepts of mental agreement and unconditional commitment. I consider myself of having a lot of faith. It has been tested from time to time throughout the years. I recall while in the Army I was told that my unit to include myself was going to be deployed to Iraq and to expect contact with the terrorist Army, (the enemy).

I look back at my experience in Iraq, I called on God many times. I was stressed and overly concerned yet highly alert because so much was happening, and so many soldiers were being killed. I needed to train and learn everything I could every minute to survive this Iraqi war. We went on an exceedingly long mission and triggered several IEDs (improvised explosive devices) while escorting dignitaries on unprotected side roads and highways. Although I practice control over stress, I was anxious to know that God controls life or death, and that's a tall order to understanding what faith is about. We needed to be able to trust God and pray that things will work out. Without an institution of faith, soldiers can get lost in the spiritual combat grounds of war.

I kept the faith and prayed every day and night to keep my mind from going nuts fighting back a wave of emotions. I needed to concentrate on the mission to stay alive. I realize faith is for the trustworthy and believer. Having faith requires a solid grounding in whatever it is that I am investing my energy. Faith contains an element of confidence that may not be present in belief. Although I have healed my major emotional wounds, the reactions they left behind continue to be triggered by critical moments that I need to process. They are now easier and faster to resolve with loving acceptance.

I had to learn that when we believe the truth with enough self-assurance to act, we use faith. It does not take much faith to see enormous things happen, even amazing things. We often spend time and energy trying to intensify our faith when Jesus said that's not our problem. We pray and ask God, pleading for him to give us more faith. So, for me to have faith, I must hear or read God's promises in the bible.

Faith does not come by fasting or praying for it or even having someone lay hands on you to present it. It only comes from hearing God's Word letting it saturate your mind. Once you hear it, you still must choose to believe it. The bottom line, faith, and belief that comes from reading and nourishing from the Word of God will soon lead you to start praying differently than prayers of people who don't believe God. Prayers to God are different period! God has not run out of muscle or out of power. That is one thing you comprehend as you spend time with God through your Bible. God hasn't run out of power, some people just run out of faith. In (Romans 12:2 KJV) we must allow the Holy Spirit to renew our minds by the Word of God. For example, when we grow in spiritual understanding, we learn how to discharge our faith.

Therefore, it is so important for people to read the bible, to get filled with faith, and then act on that faith. I know it is hard for some people to sit and read but it is so important to get in the habit of reading God's word and his promises. Talk with your Pastor, Minister, or Deacon for extra assurance because your life is only as restricted as your faith in God. If you don't like what you're in acknowledgment of, then grow into the Word of God and change what you're believing! The variation in life comes from the faith in God that a person uses to discharge his power through the body. That is what pushes a person to victory…faith in God! To believe is to receive something. To have faith is to know that something is.

Because we live in a domain of manner and substance, the action is the physical relation to having what you want. Every time you are willing to take a risk, you increase your ability to trust and believe in yourself.

Let's move onto Chapter 7.

Chapter 7

Quitting is not an Option

Have you ever failed at something, don't have enough to make it, and have come to a point that you just want to quit? Have you admitted to yourself that you wanted to throw in the towel? For those of you who believe that you are not good enough, you need to know that God has a word for you. It may or may not make you feel good, but it is good for you. He knows that you are tired and discouraged. He wants you to know that there are dangers in quitting and that you are better and stronger than you think.

In the bible, Job lost everything, and to add more, his friends started to turn on him and wonder why all this happened. Job's friends said it was because he had hidden sin in his life. From (Job 4-37 KJV), Job defends his position against his friends and his wife, as to why he remains dedicated to the Lord. Through the middle of his bad situation, Job says, "Though He slays me, yet will I trust him. Even so, I will defend my ways before him."

So, no matter what happens in your life, you must be like Job and hang in there for the long road ahead. God starts to reveal himself and his intention to Job. He asks Job; "who are you to question me about what I allow you to go through in life?" Meanwhile, God is answering Job's question to him. After Job rebukes his friends, God reestablished Job's fortunes. The Bible says he received double of everything that he had, why? Because he did not give up, he believed in God. Job emphasizes to us in fact that in the worst of hardships, that Quitting Is Not an Option.

Just like Job, some of us had hardships in our lives. As for myself, I've lost a lot during my addiction, self-esteem, dignity, respect, self-confidence, and assurance.

During my addiction, I never thought about how it would affect my family, the people around me, or how it affects me. I never owned it. I never cared. Therefore, the outcome caused me to lose everything just like Job. It took me some time to realize that I was losing everything, so I forced myself to pay attention to my life, where it was heading, and what my future was going to look like if I did not get help. I tried Rehabilitation, but I did not work the program because I was only there to make everyone happy. Again, I had to understand that I would not have a chance at a normal life if I did not stop this madness.

God was and still the driving force in my life. I just needed to be with him, talk to him, listen to him, and then everything came together. Yes, there were times I thought God was unaware or uninterested in my distress. But God can be trusted, not because he proved over and over, he has power and authority but because he proved many times over that he is God. You might feel as though you are in a storm. Your family may be feuding, money may be tight, you feel discouraged in church, or you feel isolated and lonely. What can calm your storm is to trust and believe that God hears your cry, and he will do what he said he will do. Just don't quit because we serve a progressive and dynamic God.

There is a purpose behind everything you go through, and that quitting is not an option. (Job 1:12 KJV) states The LORD said to Satan, "Very well, then, everything he has is in your power, but on the man, himself do not lay a finger.

Some of us are going through different issues or situations than others, but overall, if it is an uncomfortable thing in your life that you are going through, and it is causing pain if it makes you feel bad about yourself or what you are going through or that you just want to quit. It is time to get to work. This is a cause for God to intervene, to work a miracle for you. I recall running up a credit card over $22,000.00, I was distraught, I did not think that things would get that bad, I was so upset with myself. So, I had to humble myself, get on my knees, and ask God for help. Well, a long story short: I started a process, a budget, and eventually paid the credit card off in one year. All I can say is, what a mighty God we serve. He installed a plan in my head, the energy to go forwarded, and the strength to complete the mission. God spoke and I listened. "I DID NOT QUIT".

Some individuals think they can fix their issues all by themselves. I am here to tell you, that it is impossible without God. He is like a surgeon; he can go into the area where the cancer is located, cut out the cancer, and sew you back up with no problem. We will destroy everything without a doubt. Whatever you do, do it with God and his blessing. Remember there is a blessing and testimony from whatever you are going through. God will and he can do it, he will get the Glory.

God is not going to let you have a do it your- self-project. He is not going to let you solve your issues or meet your challenges yourself. He is going to give you the strength to solve your problems. He is with you all the way. So, there is no reason why you should stop fighting because you have everything you need to be victorious, it is all accessible to you.

Instead of thinking of throwing in the towel, trust God to help you figure your problems because "Quitting is Not an Option".

Let's move go to Chapter 8

Chapter 8

Your Past is not your Future

Overcoming the past may be difficult for some, but there is one thing, you can do it. Your past is not or should not be your future. (Jeremiah 29:11 KIV) says for I know the thoughts that I think toward you, saith the Lord, thoughts of peace, and not of evil, to give you an expected end. Take his plans and make them your plans. You cannot craft those plans if you are always looking back at your past instead of God's future. His promises have your plans in them, and those treasured promises can come alive only by seeking God for them. He can give you the instructions of his word on how to get there. Don't let your past define who you are now.

Remember you cannot declare victory and be a victim at the same time. There is a choice to make. You must ignore the past and focus on your future. Walking by faith is not walking in the past. Caring for yourself to be beneficial is not pride but true humility before God. But if we walk in the light, as he is in the light, we have fellowship one with another, and the blood of Jesus Christ his Son cleanseth us from all sin (1John 1:7 KIV).

When I was 30 years old, and in the military, I recall a conversation on the phone with my mother as we talked about the troubles I used to be in when I lived at home, how terrified she was for me, how much she cried and prayed for me. She said, "don't worry about your past, it is over, move forward, do not worry about what you've done in the past, do not look back, and don't let your past ruin your future, because, God has your back". I stood by those words through the storms of my military career, it made sense and it carried me through the "feel sorry for myself" phase.

The enemy will try to use your past to destroy your future. He does not play fair or doesn't play at all…If you can walk through your past, I want you to be able to tell the story of your past as a testimony, and a blessing to others. Once I re-dedicated my life to Christ I was on fire for God. Guess what? Here comes Satan using one of my old friends, ex-friends, so-called friends, and family to throw my past sins in my face and try to make me feel guilty about my past. In Christ, we are a new creation as stated in (2 Corinthians 5:17 KJV). We have become our authentic identity in Him. Loved and forgiven, we no longer condemned as it is said in (Ephesians 1:7-9 KJV). When we have guilt over our past sins, it weighs us down, restricts us, and leads to disgrace.

Allowing guilt to define us, leads us down the wrong path. Allowing the past to stay present allows hurtful memories and bad choices to blend in our brains giving us bad behaviors while affecting people. This leads us down the road to spiritually immobilizing the atmosphere. So why don't we toss things out in our past that hinder us?

When the devil keeps directing you to look at your past, there must be something terrific in your future that he does not want you to see. Multiple times, temptation wants you to believe that you are not worthy of God's love because you are unclean, but God says repeatedly that He will forever forgive his children. God will forever give you a new start, despite the consequences of your past. Every morning we get an opportunity to be different. God's proposals for you will always be larger than your sins. God has an incredible and magnificent future planned and tailored for you. You are required to listen to Him and follow the glorious path that He has paved just for you. God has a purpose for our lives, not despite our past but because of it.

In the Bible, Saul was a murderer who tormented Christians. When he was saved by Jesus Christ, he was washed of his sins and given a brand-new name, Paul. He became one of God's best disciples. God is not ashamed of you for your past. Your past is something that identifies who you are. Your battles and the devil's compulsions you have given into before are experiences that make you stronger in your faith today. Therefore, never let your mistakes past or present take you away from God. Now that the slate is wiped clean, and you have the chance to make a turnaround. It is time for you to get it right.

"For he has rescued us from the dominion of darkness and brought us into the kingdom of the Son he loves, in whom we have redemption, the forgiveness of sins" (Colossians 1:13-14 KIV).

You never have to worry about your past sins being held against you because they are forgiven completely.

Let's go to Chapter 9

Chapter 9

In Your Darkest Hour of Need

When in the hour of the utmost need, we know not where to look for aid when days and nights of anxious thought nor help nor counsel yet have brought, then is our comfort this alone that we may meet before your throne; To you, O faithful God, we cry for rescue in our misery. For you have promised, Lord, to listen to your children's cries in time of need.

Have you ever reached that place where your relationships or anything else where you previously put your hope just wasn't enough? Maybe it is while lying in a hospital bed with an illness, witnessing a loved one facing death, or feeling abandon by someone you cared deeply for. I call it hitting rock bottom. At that moment we realize we need God. Some people offer to sit down and talk with you, others say they will pray for you. However, it is when God's presence is very much invited. But some of us reject God.

Behold, I will do a new thing, now it shall spring forth; shall you not know it? I will even make a road in the wilderness and rivers in the desert." (Isaiah 43:18-19 KIV).

"Therefore, if anyone is in Christ, he is a new creation; old things have passed away; behold, all things have become new" (2 Corinthian 5:17 KIV).

Have mercy on me, O God, have mercy on me, for in you my soul takes refuge. I will take refuge in the shadow of your wings until the disaster has passed. I cry out to God Most High, to God, who fulfills his purposes for me" (Psalms 57:1-2 KIV).

Most of us have this feeling in our hearts that we are moving towards an unusual time in all of history. In the last year in 2020, we've experienced a COVID-19 pandemic that killed over 500,000 people, and more will, unfortunately, die before we beat this. Protests erupted around the nation over the unfortunate death of Breonna Taylor and George Floyd but in our darkest need God will conquer, we will get the victory.

What you read only in fiction books is now happening right before our eyes. We cannot escape it. It's here and only going to escalate as time goes on, but we as God's children do not have to live in fear or setback. As an alternative, we need to move higher and find that place of peace in the center of God. He is our defense and sanctuary in the storm. As in the days of Noah, people are living life as if no hurricane, tornado, or racial pressure will come. It is happening before our eyes, but life goes on and so many want to live in denial and make-believe that Jesus is not coming soon. They continue to live as if there is no importance about the hour in which we are living they eat, drink, and be merry.

There must be a purpose in this. It's time to construct our ark for the storm which is already upon us. It's time to rise and talk to God in prayer. God will help you to build your ark and prepare your shelter for the future. We must learn to focus on the middle of God's peace and presence as the storm clouds come.

(Matthew 10:19 KIV) says, but when they deliver you up, take no thought how or what ye shall speak: for it shall be given you in that same hour what ye shall speak.

We are encouraged to approach the throne of God at any time especially during our hour of need. As the world crumbles and threatens to collapse, our God remains unchanged. It's amazing to grasp God's throne of grace with faith, so that we may receive mercy and find grace to help us in our time of need."

Our need leads us to prayer, which leads us to a level of the highest. We need God every hour and we need him to show us a powerful degree of need. If we don't pray, we must plead with God to teach us. And his answer likely will not be a new method but a keen awareness of our distressing need. And when he does this for us it is a precious gift to us. It is key to not destroying our lives. Constant awareness of our needs leads to constant prayer. And the constant practice of praying will teach us the importance of prayer. And constant prayer leads to a breakthrough.

Do not be afraid or embarrassed to call on the Lord. He knows that you are struggling. He saw my storms bearing down on me. At a time in my life, our bills were overwhelming, one of our kids was in trouble failing school, our home, and the car needed repairs. Without God, I was destined to continue to struggle. Even in your darkest hour, you can be encouraged as I am. Know that God is with you every step of the way, and He will deliver you from your troubles, no matter how great they were.

When I was selling drugs in the streets, partying hard, and being in promiscuous relationships, driving under the influence, and lying to family members and friends I knew I was wrong; I knew I needed to do better. In my darkest hour, I had to call on the Lord because I was heading down a troubled path. Either you are or know someone who has been or is going down a path of destruction needs God's help. Believe me, the issue will not get better until it is recognized and dealt with immediately. In your darkest hour call on the Lord, he will answer.

Let's go to Chapter 10.

Chapter 10

Being Used by God

The first thing we must do is to take self-inventory of ourselves and ask ourselves while looking into the mirror what do you see? Well, you have eyes, ears, hands, feet a mind, and a voice. Most importantly you have a heart and that is enough. Now ask yourself, "Let's see what God can use".

When I first realized I was being used by God was when I was asked to sing a song to replace someone who could not be present at a church program I was attending. I was nervous at first but then the spirit saturated me with joy. From there it was a blooming sensation to please God. I did not know at that time I was being used by God, as months go by as I continue to participate more in the church, I couldn't say no when being asked to do something for church events or programs.

I was eager to do it. I never thought about being used by God until someone approached me and said, "continue to let God use you", I stood still for a moment thinking to myself, "that makes sense, God is using me". And today, as a minister, I am more involved and love the idea of being used by God and as a leader, I want to help others to be usable by God.

You were planned for God's pleasure and formed just for him. The purpose for which God made you is created to become like Christ, molded for service, and made for Spiritual War. David served God's purpose in his generation. We must be strong and very courageous. God wants to use a specific person at a specific time to reach a0 specific person. You don't have to be a perfect person, but you do have to have a pure heart. In (2

Timothy 2:21 KJV), it states: "If a man, therefore, purges himself from these, he shall be a vessel unto honor, sanctified, and meet for the master's use, and prepared unto every good work."

God uses all types of people. He uses bold people, shy people, different races, ages, backgrounds, and stages of life. But there is one thing that God will not use: He will not use a dirty vessel. You must be clean on the inside. How do you cleanse yourself? You do it through a humble word: confession. Therefore, (1 John 1:9 KJV) states, "If we confess our sins, he is faithful and just and will forgive us our sins and purify us from all unrighteousness." If one wants to be used by God: They should take the time to sit down with a pen and paper, and say, "Ok God, what's wrong in my life?" Show me. Then write it down, and I will acknowledge it. I will confess it to you." When God gives you the thought, write it down. It works because I did it.

When you can say in the previous years, "I work for God, and now it is easy to walk with God". Then you have grown 20 years mature in faith. The known prophetess, Anna, of the New Testament. She was merely a widow who walked with God, serving Him in the temple day and night. Then one day Jesus unexpectedly presented himself in the temple, and Anna used that opportunity to show others the Messiah. Thus, Samuel in the Old Testament was serving God day and night in the temple. Samuel merely wanted to know the Lord, and converse with Him.

Saul (Paul) and Barnabas were simply resident ministers at the First Church of Antioch, although they were serving the Lord in fasting and prayer, the Holy Spirit spoke to the Church that they should isolate these two men apart. Together these two men would plant some of the first Churches in the Gentile world, and one would go on to write a great portion of the New Testament.

The thing they all had in common were the characteristic that defined them not only from the beginning, but also to the end, and that was their forward example of walking with God. A sinful past does not suggest we can't be used by God. Your sinful past will frequently empower you to be used more effectively by God. He will use you no matter what you did in the past. Sometimes it will cause problems with people who know about your past and who will refuse to believe you have changed. Don't let it trouble you. The dilemma is not yours any longer, it is theirs. If they decide to not see how you have changed, then they are the losers. They have lost the opportunity to know the new you.

I've been in the same situation when my friends and family members treated me differently because they cannot believe that I've changed, after a dreadful past. They have it in their mind that someone that has had an addiction past could not overcome and could not be used by God. Do as I have done, prove them wrong. Nevertheless, make the decision that God can use you because of what you have done. Just give yourself to Him and you will be astonished what He can do through you! It seems the more I seek God's will in my life the weirder I have appeared to my friends and relatives who may or may not be seeking His will.

Family and friends won't try to understand. It is easier to just slap the label "RIDICULOUS" on you and then proceed to talk about you with others. So, (John 15:18-19 KJV) says "If the world hates you, ye know that it hated me before it hated you. If ye were of the world, the world would love his own: but because ye are not of the world, but I have chosen you out of the world, therefore the world hateth you."

You have been chosen to be used because you can handle it. You must choose to jump in all the way and engage yourself in what God would have you to be accomplishing.

Chapter Eleven is waiting for you.

Chapter 11

Embrace your
Identity in Christ

For reasons, some people frequently unsure about who we are because we use other's thinking as our point of reference. What we do is often measured and judged by them either as acceptable or unacceptable and we allow our performance to define us. So, who does God say you are currently that you are in Christ? How does He see you from the time when you have been born again spiritually? Related to the Bible, you are God's child, a co-inheritor with Christ, a Saint with a new life, a member of the body of Christ, and a resident of His kingdom. Your identity in Christ is unquestionable you belong to God, and He cares profoundly about you!

However, the only dependable source of our identity is God! He created us, loves us, sent His son Jesus Christ to die for us, and transforms our lives through His Holy Spirit! In truth, now we receive Jesus as our Savior and Lord, we are born again spiritually, and our identity is drastically changed. (2 Corinthians 5:17 KJV) says, therefore, if anyone is in Christ, the new creation has come: The old has vanished, the new is here! Discovering and accepting your identity in Christ can be an invigorating and daunting experience!

The following concepts and scripture passages will strengthen your understanding of the identity you have in Christ (Knowing you've accepted Jesus Christ as your Lord and Savior).

(Ephesians 2:10 KJV) says, for we are his workmanship, created in Christ Jesus unto good works, which God hath before ordained that we should walk in them.

(1 John 3:1 KJV) says: See what great love the Father has lavished on us, that we should be called children of God! And that is what we are! The reason the world does not know us is that it did not know him.

If you investigate the secret lives of people in all categories of life, you find individuals who try to look big on the outside but crying deeply for love on the inside. A worldwide problem is not being able to love ourselves the way that God loves us. Most of us do not do this well. Our lives are often filled with anxiety, concern, and depression because we listen to the lies of the enemy instead of God's truth. So many have misplaced their identity, yes misplaced, and do not know who they are. Misplaced it and they need to find it and get it back. To successfully fulfill God's will in our lives without distress and concern, we must have a precise view of ourselves and know our identity in Christ.

(Hebrews 4:12 KJV) says for the word of God is alive and active. Sharper than any two-edged sword, it penetrates even to dividing soul and spirit, joints, and marrow; it judges the thoughts and attitudes of the heart. His words uncover what is in our hearts. That is why we need to meditate on it day and night. It separates between what is in the soul (our inner part containing our mind, passion, and will with which we contact all the things of the emotional realm) and what is spirit (our deepest part with which we contact God and confirm all the things of the spiritual realm). Most people are guided by their souls. They make plans with their mind exclusively, they are led by their reactions, and will do whatever they wish.

Our identity in Christ also means we belong to God's kingdom. (Philippians 3:20 KJV) tells us, " For our conversation is in heaven; from whence also we look for the Saviour, the Lord Jesus Christ. Because we haven't tangibly moved out of the earthly kingdom, it is easy to have confused thoughts. However, we now serve a unique King. We are citizens of a new-found Kingdom. And as such, we must be careful to initiate our loyalty where it is rightfully due. When you see yourself as Christ sees you, others may begin to see you that way also. If you are stable and secure in your identity in Him, your accomplishments, speech, and life will express God's love. You may find more opportunities to share the gospel, and Christ will be more glorified.

With your identity in Christ comes a responsibility: We must now live our lives following whom we've become through Christ. We've been made clean, blessed, and righteous in God's eyes, but we are still human so, we still can sin. To live untainted lives, we must embrace our identity in Christ on a day-to-day basis. This includes holding on to the truths about whom he says you are, he created you after all in his image. We are children of the king and there is nothing anyone can do or say to change that.

Throughout the day, we are continuously criticizing ourselves with negativity that we don't entirely measure up to. How about changing the radio station? Instead of listening to the same bombarding messages repeatedly, just tune in to the word of God for positive strengthening messages of your worth. It is so important to find that innermost positive spirited energy. Some of us place our identity in labels, whether it is in our careers or our relationships. But what happens when you lose that special person and that job? Who better to place our identity in than one who never changes, the one who loves us unconditionally? Christ! Popularity fades but there is one who will never change that we can hold on to, Christ!

Be rooted in your identity in Christ. Write some scriptures in a journal. Make a wallpaper of sticky notes of bible verses. Just be you and creative and be confident in being you in the spirit. Remember we need to learn from one another, no man is an island embracing Christ with each other is the ultimate additive to claim your crown.

Let's read on to Chapter 12, "Equipped with The Armor of God".

Chapter 12

Equipped with the Armor of God

In our warfare with Satan, his culture, and our human flaws, we need spiritual support. God provides the powerful armor of God to protect us and provide us with victory! The Armor of God described by the Apostle Paul in (Ephesians 6:10-18 KJV) is our spiritual defense against attacks by Satan. Every day, all day an invisible war erupts around you by this clever, diabolical enemy (Satan) who seeks to wreak havoc on everything that matters to you, your emotions, your mind, your family, your future. Although undetectable, the armor of God is real, and when utilized correctly and worn daily, it provides solid protection against the enemy's attacks. After these attacks, you will still be standing. So, stand firm, stand your ground.

The Armor of God is a metaphor in the bible (Ephesians 6:10-18 KJV) that reminds Christians about the reality of spiritual battle and describes the shelter, the protection available to them. The full armor of God that Christians are called to put on contains the Belt of Truth, the Breastplate of Righteousness, the Gospel of Peace, the Shield of Faith, the Helmet of Salvation, and the Sword of the Spirit. With all the protection in the bible, we must keep the faith, be strong in the Lord and his mighty power Stand firm with the belt of truth buckled around our waist. The assurance is that we exist for God. He created us for His purposes and has equipped every believer to serve Him in some manner.

"We are His workmanship, created in Christ for good works, which God prepared beforehand so that we would walk in them". Everything about us has been created by God to equip us for the work He destined long before our birth. A prayer warrior takes part in that battle through prayer interceding for others and praying for God's will to be done in all things. We know that there is a great spiritual battle ongoing now more than ever (Ephesians 6:12 KJV).

How does the Lord respond to Satan's enticements? "When we are made righteous through faith in Christ, we are continuously made right with God. So many of Satan's strikes are redirect by knowing that we are righteous in the eyes of God. When we are tempted to doubt who God is, negotiate the gospel, leave our spiritual duties, or decide for ourselves what is and is not sinful, our response must be, "it is written."

We must be on the alert while having our defenses up launching a full-blown attack to send Satan running! A person wearing the armor of God is not slack or insensitive to the forces that he knows will come. He is expecting an attack; he is observant! In (Ephesians 6:10-20 KJV), Paul talks about putting on the whole armor of God. In the book of Ephesians was one of Paul's letters written from prison. During his time in prison, he became well acquainted with the armor worn and carried by his captors in the Roman army. Ensuing Isaiah's lead (Isaiah 59:17 KJV), Paul elicited a powerful similarity between a soldier's armor and the spiritual armor of God. You see, we don't have to be discouraged by Satan's power. Remember we aren't in this battle alone. We have access to the greatest power in the universe!

Throughout my journey a need to be equipped with the Armor of God was essential. I left myself open to Satan's attacks. I grew up in Maryland, after graduating high school I hung out spending time smoking, drinking, getting into fights, and just being in the streets. Weeks go by after getting off work I continued to experiment with different drugs with random people around. Convincing myself I was overweight I then began abusing diet pills. I shifted slowly drifting away from work and having fun, to focusing on nothing else but how messed up could I get in a night. I had no idea the kind of inferno I was playing with. I thought it was harmless and just having fun. At some point it got profoundly serious I lost touch with this enthusiastic and talented person I was. I didn't care about anything.

After returning home from a party, wasted, as usual, I passed out on the floor next to my bed and did not remember driving home and how I miss the bed and ended on the floor was beyond me. When I woke up, I had no memory of the night before, the look of honor on my face in the mirror was priceless. I would hope no one call to tell me what I had done. This was something I will never forget. Long story short, I enrolled in a drug rehab center, completed the 60-day program than 10 months later with the blessing of my mother, I joined the Army 21 years later I retired.

Years after experiencing my life spiraling downhill, today I felt compelled to share my story so that someone knows that they are not alone, and their life is precious therefore cherish it and most of all equip yourself with the Coat of Armor of God to shield you with protection from Satan's antics. I was blessed to be able to connect to my life again knowing that Satan's attack was not successful. I am moving on, still blessed, and equipped with the Armor of God. "For our struggle is not against flesh and blood, but against the rulers, against the authorities, against the powers of this dark world and the spiritual forces of evil in the heavenly realms" (Ephesians 6:12 KIV).

Paul wants people to understand why they need the armor. He was advocating the idea that the devil is alive and well on planet earth and will take every chance to attack us. His goal is to lure us away from God and destroy us. When I became a Christian, I heard the phrase "spiritual warfare" and the theory of unseen forces at work made me anxious. But the more I learned and experienced God, the more I saw His powers. The truth is that God has given me, given us the victory, even if we couldn't see the battle. So, don't take your life for granted use it to help someone seek God, enjoy his love, and understand his promises.

Chapter 13 awaits!!!!!!

Chapter 13

Choosing Faith over Fear

Our world seems to be in a nonstop state of war and crisis. The job market is depressing, natural disasters create destruction, and stories of crime lead the headlines. As Christians, we know that fear should have no room in our lives, but how can we disregard what's going on around us? It's a choice every believer can't escape either we are walking in faith or fear. To build our faith, we must broaden our application of God's word, knowledge, and understanding.

It's impossible to instantaneously trust God than not trust God. Therefore, you cannot both obey and disobey Him, with partial obedience and disobedience. So, which road are you traveling? As you walked through this season of a worldwide pandemic, have you sensed God's closeness, or have you questioned why He is so silent regarding the concerns you? If you have been calm in recent months, have you ever felt like God didn't care that you were in the middle of terrible conditions? In any case, what condition were you in that left you feeling alone and unnoticed?

Some Christians who read the Bible and believe in God still choose to live with fear. They See others experience hardship and despair they start to wonder if it could happen to them: For example, someone died in an accident I could die too, or someone may rob this bank while I am in it. This kind of rationality places your circumstances above your connection to God. If we allow Satan to get us to think like this, he has won the battle for our minds. But when you concentrate on God rather than your conditions, whatever the situation is, you have won.

I opened the news app on my phone, and it triggered a surge of stress as I cautiously waited for what news is coming next. It is almost like being in the military deployed, the stress continues. With God, we don't have to be flooded by our fears. Jesus tells us not to let our hearts be afraid or allow ourselves to be anxious and disturbed. We are not victims of our fear it is a normal reaction, but we must control fear with faith and not let fear control our hearts. We don't have to wait for perfect situations to have no fear. When we seek God during our darkest hour, we will be delivered from our fears. So, don't worry choose "faith over fear".

Though your future is uncertain, it's never uncertain to God. Hold on to Him and He will take you where you need to be. You are destined for victory. Continue to place your eyes on Jesus, the pioneer, and perfecter of faith. (Hebrews 12:2 KIV). Fear will cause rejection, procrastination, and uncertainty. Faith enables you to face your enemy, face your vulnerability, face your challenges, and then fight them knowing that your God is greater than anything standing in front of you. Don't mistake faith for fear.

We will march away from this pandemic. It will not be easy. This virus is deadly and dangerous. Yes, cherished people are losing their lives to this virus every day. Even now that there is a vaccine, some are afraid with fear and will not take it, so they are not protected. I am not dismissing the seriousness of this problem, but we must not be consumed with fear, grief, and panic those things won't protect us. We must face the crisis but most importantly focus on God, there is an answer. That's faith! God gave us common sense to deal with this coronavirus pandemic in every way that we can. Scientists, doctors, and experts are giving us essentially minute-by-minute information on ways to fight the spread of this coronavirus and flatten the turn to bring a faster end to this shock. We are living in a time where we have more cures, more medicine, better technology, and greater science than we've ever had. People are living twice as long as generations ago. When you look at this pandemic against the background of history, there is still so much to be grateful for.

(Matthew 10:26–31 KJV) says, have no fear of them, for nothing is covered that will not be revealed, or hidden that will not be known. What I tell you in the dark, say in the light, and what you hear whispered, proclaim on the housetops. And do not fear those who kill the body but cannot kill the soul. Rather fear him who can destroy both soul and body. Are not two sparrows sold for a penny? And not one of them will fall to the ground apart from your Father. But even the hairs of your head are all numbered. Fear not, therefore; you are of more value than many sparrows.

God does not judge you for your feelings. Our feelings and reactions to situations are as rare as we are. There is no right or wrong when it comes to your feelings. We can't make an inclination when moving forward or dealing with something if we choose to ignore it. When we choose faith over fear God is not surprised by our "extraordinary times"! We can choose faith over fear today because no matter "how unstable our situation is" Faith over fear is defeated on the cross which secured those who are in Christ for today, we don't have to worry because the best is yet to come!

When I was in my teenaged years I was confused and fearful of not knowing my future. I knew I was a child of God, a believer but I did not know how to connect with God like I see some teens today. This caused great concern for me because I was going down the wrong path. Everything I do was not of God. I fear myself; I had no faith. Although my future was uncertain, I needed to let God be my future. Though I slipped away from the church, "I knew that I needed help and I realized that I needed God. Whether we conceal our fear of being brave or tiptoe away to seek refuge, it can have a powerful effect on our decisions, actions and, thinking. Keep the faith and lose the fear.

Take a deep breath and continue to Chapter 14

Chapter 14

Embracing your Storm, During Difficult Times

There are not many things that we can count on in this unstable life. We can count on storms to arrive. We can also count on God's frequent and unshakable power for those storms. When difficult times come, when terrible things happen, we do not have to ponder where God is. Instead, we can hold on to the word that is found in (Jeremiah 16:19 KIV), "Lord, you are my strength and my protection you are a safe place for me to run in times of trouble".

Our storms might look different to each of us, but they all can change us forever. God is the only one who has the power to take what seems catastrophic and destructive and turn it around for good. It may not happen as rapidly as we'd like, it may feel like a battle; we might find ourselves craving for another way, but blessing will come from it. For it's simply the way God works. No matter what storm rages in your life, no matter how intense the winds or how elevated the waves may be, where you are today is no surprise to God, he is responsible. Keep your mind on Him and look upon the uncontrolled waters. Embrace Him and He will supply everything you need to stand strong in the storm.

We may wake any morning and raging storms seem to create havoc in our lives. Whether we suffer heartbreak, tragedy, or a rough time dealing with everyday strains, storms will come, and they will go. And while we wish they would leave more rapidly than they arrive, it may help to acknowledge the magnitude of the unavoidable severe downpours we often experience. God never promised us that life would be easy, but He does promise that He will always work for our good and that He is greater than any storm we face in this world, even in places where we can't see. He is with us during our walk through the storm. None of us are exempt from facing storms, but we need to trust the word of God even in the midst of those storms!

Let's say everything we need has been stripped away. You lose your job. You are failing all your classes. Your home feels like a combat zone. You have been diagnosed with a serious illness. Your church is in desperate channels. In seasons like this, many of us (myself included) feel like we need something new, a word from God that applies directly to our situation. God gives us this strength while saturating us with his grace and mercy.

I can say there were many storms in my life, each storm was of a different magnitude and required a special kind of prayer for that situation. Bottom line, I knew a breakthrough would be coming soon because I never gave up on God. We all are children of God, he loves us, and that we are not alone. I invite you to see that God can lighten your burdens and be the protection you are seeking. We need to help each other find the protection that they so desire. That protection will help us resist the storms of life. There is no doubt in my heart that if we seek God's help, we will be protected from Satan's work.

As we face the storms of life, I know that if we make our best effort and depend upon Jesus we will be blessed with the comfort, strength, temperance, and peace that we are seeking, with confidence in our hearts that at the end of our time here on earth, we will hear the words of the Master: "Well done, thou good and faithful servant.

During my storm, I allowed envy and anger to sidetrack me. Therefore, I know I must allow God to restore my life and heal me or I will not last. Through it all, I know my life is truly a testimony and that it's not about me, it's about him. The following scriptures explore the spirit of Jesus and his power to overcome our storms.

(Philippians 1:6 KJV) " Being confident of this very thing, that he which hath begun a good work in you will perform it until the day of Jesus Christ."

(Isaiah 41:10 KJV) "Fear thou not; for I am with thee: be not dismayed; for I am thy God: I will strengthen thee; yea, I will help thee; yea, I will uphold thee with the right hand of my righteousness."

(John 10:27-28 KJV) " My sheep hear my voice, and I know them, and they follow me:

And I give unto them eternal life; and they shall never perish, neither shall any man pluck them out of my hand".

The Bible says that "Even though I walk through the valley of the shadow of death, I will fear no evil, for you are with me; your rod and your staff, they comfort me." To have peace during our storms we need to trust in God's Word, do not let fear have its way, be confident of God's goodness, and recognize that God is in control.

If you are going through a storm, do not be fearful. Jesus is your shelter. He is in control! If you are going through a family or financial difficulty, let me tell you, Jesus is your provider! If you are suffering from any sickness, remember, Jesus is your healer! If you are depressed, please know that Jesus will be on your cheering team, because Jesus is your lifeline!

You may be in a season right now where everything around you seems out of control. It could be your job, your family, or your finances. You may be troubled about what's happening in our nation. When life seems to be tumbling downhill, even the just can get disturbed. The bible says. "But the fruit of the Spirit is love, joy, peace" (Galatians 5:22 KJV). This comes from the fruit of the Spirit, not what the world can give. Nevertheless, you cannot have true, long-lasting peace in your life until first, you become a child of God until you're saved.

It is the peace of God that passes all understanding, to rule your heart and mind. This kind of peace is not the nonexistence of complications. It is the addition of power and strength. Jesus' disciples had to experience it to learn it, and you will, too. "Thou wilt keep him in perfect peace, whose mind is stayed on thee: because he trusteth in thee" (Isaiah 26:3 KJV).

Chapter 15

You Matter to God

I used to feel like I was just a face in a crowd or identified by my social security number. Recently I went to the doctor's office, I took a number, sat down, and was called by that number. I felt depersonalized and dehumanized, then I realized that is exactly how the devil wanted me to feel that I did not matter much to anyone, especially to God. Wrong!!! You matter to God! He knows precisely what you are going through and why you are heartbroken. He sees you, understands you, and most importantly cares for you, he calls you by name. You matter to God, your life matter to God.

Through many obstacles, and hardship we've experienced may seem like the evidence that the Lord doesn't care, but this is not true. Some of the best Saints in Christian history have experienced indescribable suffering without doubting God's love for them. Although the Lord has not assured us an easy life, even in the middle of our problems we can know with assurance that our lives matter to Him. Below are two of my favorite scriptures that I think to describe how God feels about you and me.

I waited patiently for the Lord, He heard my cry and inclined to me. He brought me up out of the pit of destruction, out of the miry clay, and He set my feet upon a rock making my footsteps firm. He put a new song in my mouth, a song of praise to our God; many will see and fear and will trust in the Lord (Psalm 40:1-3 KJV).

The Lord appeared "I have loved you with an everlasting love; therefore, I have drawn you with lovingkindness" (Jeremiah 31:3 KJV).

Before the universe was created, God had you in mind, and for His purposes. These purposes will extend far beyond the limited years you will spend on earth. You were made to last endlessly because you are not an accident, you matter to God. I would like to tell you who you are. In truth, let me declare who you are! The Bible says you are an heir of God and a co-heir with Christ. You have a crown that will last indefinitely. Jesus gives us strength and power to do incredible things, and when we perform within His will and for His purpose, we cannot fail. Clearly said, we exist, we matter because God made us.

God has placed a purpose inside of you to better his kingdom. Each one of us can contribute to his kingdom. We have gifts that God has given to us because we matter to him. My purpose, my talent may be different from yours, it's like adding different seasonings in a particular meal to bring out the good taste. We are special to God because we add a different purpose, a different talent to God's kingdom. God said we are the reason He created the universe!

Until we experience the presence of God in our lives, it is hard to feel like we matter to Him. If you have never experienced God's presence, your time will come, and it will be exciting, trust me. God does love you so very much that he gave his only begotten son, yes, you've heard it before, but can you imagine that? For us? I pray you will understand how much you matter to Him.

Making the mistake that God is too busy taking care of the "big things" instead of the little problems they are facing is untrue. Are you one? It may be your child marking on the walls of the house, a mouse got into your house, or the small pimple on your face. No matter how minor it sounds, if it concerns you, then God wants to take care of it! God intends to take care of every area of your life, even the tiniest detail. He loves you so much that He knows the number of hairs you have on your head. And if God is interested in the insignificant details of your life, then you do not have to conquer any problem on your own.

Throughout my life occupying the dirty streets, my drug interactions, my military career, retirement, my cancer crisis, and the multiple medications I am taking daily, God has been there for me. The journey has been rough at times, through it all God has been there on my good days, bad days, and every day in between, He is always there to listen to my burdens. We made it through the year 2020, not a date that I even thought possible back in 1972 when I was ten-year-old growing up in Landover, Maryland. I am grateful that during this season of uncertainty and a tremendous sense of not being safe God was with me! Because I matter to him.

The most vital thing you can know in life is that God loves you, the most essential thing you can do in life is love him back. That's what makes us different from animals, nature, and the galaxy. God provides us with choices! He lets us choose what to do with our lives, what to be, and who to love.

So, the next time someone forgets to invite you, steals your parking spot or doesn't notice your presence, take heart. Be reminded. You matter to God and me because we are connected. God knows exactly what you are going through and where you are hurting. Because you matter to God. He calls you by name. He sees you and cares for you, just as He cared for the people when He first walked on earth.

A short story in the Bible "Jesus needed to go through Samaria" to get from Judea to Galilee (John 4:4 KJV). During Jesus's day, any Jew would have taken a different and longer route to avoid going through Samaria because they hated the Samaritans, although the way through Samaria took less time. But Jesus intentionally took the shorter, evaded route, just so He could stop by Samaria to talk to the woman who had been searching for something in her life to fulfill her.

This woman had five husbands and the man she was living with was not her husband. Things were not going right in her life. She was possibly looking for answers and satisfaction and must have felt regretful about her failed marriages and current lifestyle therefore in (John 4:28–29 KJV) despite all this, she mattered to Jesus! He wanted to go to her and minister to her. And certainly, after she met Jesus, the perfect Man, she was changed. She was no longer ashamed and went into the city to tell the people about Him.

Remember You Matter to GOD !

Chapter 16

Your Relationship with God Defines You

The significance of your life's purpose is so that God can use you while you're here on Earth for training created for eternity. God wants us to create a relationship with him by trusting in him. How? When you want to engage in a relationship with a significant other, time must be or should be spent to show that you want to invest that opportunity to get to know them. Devoting your time with God, talking to him, reading his word, is the best way to cultivate a relationship with God. Question? How are you going to ask God for a blessing, to heal you, to assist you with your family or finances if you don't know him? God knows if we are genuine. Our relationship with God defines us by:

Getting to know God, you must first listen to what He has to say. Start from the beginning with the book of Genesis and gradually read your way through the end of the book of Revelations. Realizing that God loves you and that He wants to help you walk through life by walking with Him, in everyday life, and your Spirit, and remember he is always with you.

Loving God and keep His commandments, and His commandments are not grievous (1 John 5:3 KJV).

Loving thy neighbor as you love thy self. To strengthen our relationship with others is to strengthen our relationship with God. Although you cannot see God, he is all over therefore it is easy to locate that special place we call now and days the "Prayer Room" and begin to tell God what is really on your mind. We must be sincere and truthful because God knows all. We cannot deceive God. In (Genesis Chapter 3 KIV) before Adam sinned in the Garden of Eden, both he and Eve knew God on an intimate, private level. They walked with God in the garden and talked directly to him. Due to the sin of man, we became separated and disconnected from God. God has always desired to be close to us, to have a relationship with us.

We live these days in this world of limitless anxieties, and our rapid-paced lives mean that our hearts end up occupied with all types of people, experiences, and ideas, thus giving us very, little time to calm ourselves before concentrating on God, draw close to God, consider God. When our hearts are drawn away from God, and we do not obey God in our hearts, we are therefore powerless of gaining the work of the Holy Spirit, this defines who we are. When I was without God's guidance and leadership in my life, I often ended up overextended and consumed in both body and mind as I engaged myself with all the various people, experiences, and matters in my life, and nothing I did turn out well, this defined me.

Additionally, when my connection with God became normal, I experience God's supervision in all things, I can have a perspective on problems, shortcomings, and deficiencies in my daily activities in an opportune way that identifies me today. So, if we wish to achieve our goals, then we must willfully pray more to God and regularly consider God's love and grace. It is normal for Christians to feel the intimacy of a connection with God. True affection with God, which has been pursued by Christians since Christ walked the earth. But genuine intimacy with God is not only a feeling but an appropriate romantic relationship. It grows far deeper than emotion, down to our souls, and manifested by our actions. (Proverbs 3:32 KJV) says "For the LORD detests the perverse but takes the upright into his confidence". True intimacy with God begins with being close to Him.

The relationship that God chooses to have with us is embedded in love. No other verse in the Bible summarizes God's relationship with humanity and his greatest love for us. (John 3:16 KJV) explains God's perfect love for you: "For God so loved the world that He gave His only Son, that whoever believes in Him should not perish but have everlasting life". It tells us that the love God has for us, and the magnitude of that love is so great that

He surrendered his only Son on our behalf. God's love for us encourages our love for God.

God encourages us into an intimate relationship with Him: a union with Christ refers to a relationship between the disciple and Jesus Christ. There are limitless passages throughout the Bible that expose that believers are joined in Christ: God takes residence in us; In (John 15:5 KJV) it says, we are the branches and Jesus is the vine; In (1 Peter 2:4-5 KJV) says, Christ is the foundation, and we are living stones in the foundation.

Nothing is more important or crucial to knowing and enjoying God than a union with him. It is the core of our Christian faith. Jesus is residing in us and because of this, Jesus is accessible to us anytime and anywhere because we believe. This personal relationship with God is not as difficult to find as we might think, and there is no unexplained formula for getting it.

Trusting in God to get us through each day and believing that he is our maintainer is the way to have a relationship with him. When we become children of God, we receive the Holy Spirit, who will begin to operate on our hearts. We should read the Bible, join a Bible-believing church, and pray without ceasing, all these things will assist us to grow spiritually. Although we may not see changes instantly, we will start to see them over time, and all the realities will become evident.

Fellowship with God is merely conceivable through the blood of Christ. Before we are saved, we are in animosity with God. God desires to welcome you into His eternal family as his glorified child. God's Word, the Bible, is all that we need for fellowship with him. We glorify him by presenting to his will and obeying the commands included in his Word. God is light, and light cannot have fellowship with darkness.

I can honestly say that I am so glad that I have a relationship with God. I choose the time to talk, listen or just be in His presence. We must enjoy the harmony, gratification, and delight of the fellowship God has supplied us with. Just remember He shall supply all your needs according to His riches in glory.

(John 1:12 KJV and Romans 10:9 KJV) relay that we start our relationship with God by receiving His Son Jesus, believing that He is God and that He paid the price for our sins to reestablish us to a relationship with Him. (Romans 3:23 KJV and 6:23 KJV) say that we accept Jesus' death as a replacement for the penalty we should have paid for sin and His resurrection as a victory over sin and death. When we do this, we received eternal life. A personal relationship with God is based on Faith. Only God can save and restore us from Sin. Just remember, your relationship with God would be different from mine or anyone else.

Chapter 17

Stay in the Battle and Receive your Breakthrough

We all like to win first place. But we often do not lose because we do not come in first. We lose when we give up. Some Christians have given up the battle to receive their blessings on living their best lives, some are struggling to just stay faithful to God, and to his word, and to achieve spiritual stability. We have a choice we can run away, engage in it, and we can go into battle. These three things will determine a good or bad outcome. It is not up to God or a pastor. It is up to us. Generally, people do give up though, unfortunately, they give up on their faith as well because it is too difficult, and the stress is too great. We give in to the flesh because they do not feed the spirit with the Truth.

We are in times of most important evolution, and it is easy to feel stressed or doubtful. This is a time to believe that God has your best interest at hand. If you are sowing anger, opposing, doubt, and panic, then that is what you are going to reap. The Bible tells us not to get weary in doing well for at the proper time we will reap if we do not give up. The challenge for us is to weather the storm before the breakthrough.

You are closer to your breakthrough than you have ever been before! You are closer to your miracle than you even realize. I am not talking about God going to change things for you years down the road. If you are reading this right now, I want you to know that you may not understand everything that is going on in your life at the present time. Despite the fact, that Satan is hitting you hard. Despite you going through the greatest trial of your life. Despite everything going wrong in your life. Just hold on you are on the verge of a Breakthrough change is about to happen. If He said it, he will do it and if God spoke it, He will bring it to pass.

(Galatians 6:9 KJV) says, let us not become weary in doing well, for at the proper time we will reap a harvest if we do not give up.

No battle is won without a fight, there is always a battle before our breakthrough.

(Psalm 30:5 KJV)says, for his anger endureth but a moment; in his favour is life: weeping may endure for a night, but joy cometh in the morning.

Some of us are waiting for a Breakthrough in our family, in our lives, in a friend, neighbor, or coworker. I just want to encourage someone this morning that the breakthrough you have been praying for, is right around the corner. The Bible tells us not to get weary in doing well for at the proper time we will reap if we do not give up.

There were people in the bible that was in battle. Moses was used to delivering the people of Israel, but he faced and battled Pharaoh. David was used as a king, but he battled Goliath. Nehemiah was used to rebuilding the walls, but he battled opposition. Joseph was used mightily of God, but he battled haters. So, if you are in a battle right now that is a good indication, it just means that your breakthrough is right around the corner. I think we all can confess that we have matured through our struggles. So, let me say I think it is vital for us to know that strength is not born by seeing miracles, we get strength by going through the struggles. In 2020 during the year of the COVID-19 Pandemic, we have sustained some stress, disbelief, anger, and bitterness but God has protected us, he has given us a breakthrough. We should get delighted when we see spiritual beliefs in our lives. It means we are on the brink of a breakthrough. The challenge for us is to remember there is usually a battle before the breakthrough so take inventory of your spiritual gear, strap it on and get ready for spiritual warfare. God will put you in a predicament, only he can get you out. And when he gets you out of it, it should prove to you, that you know what you know about God.

The Bible tells us that our walk with God is going to be a journey of ups and downs. What we need to do is call on him day or night, ask him for help, and to receive your breakthrough. In between the mountaintops of victory, there are valleys of the shadow of death! In between the victories, there are struggles! In between the breakthroughs, there are battles! And before every breakthrough, there is a harder battle to fight.

You are about to enter the greatest season of your life. God is about to move in your family, business, church, finances, and in your personal life in a greater way than you have ever experienced in the past. Many of God's people today recognize they are about to experience a change. They know that something big and powerful is about to happen, they just do not know when, they just know it is close. I will tell you that you are closer to your breakthrough than you think! You are closer to your breakthrough than you have ever been before!

You are closer to your miracle than you realize. I am not talking about God going to change things for you years down the road. I am not talking about your miracle or breakthrough coming some time far off in the future.

You are on the edge of your miracle; you are on the edge of your breakthrough! It may be one hour, one week, one month, one year or right when you walk out of your front door. For some people, this may be the very day that you experience the breakthrough that you have been praying for! So, don't give up on God.

Next Stop Chapter 18

Chapter 18

God is Bigger than your Obstacles

Whatever you're going through in life just know that God is bigger than that. If you're going through an illness God is bigger than that, if you're going through addiction or depression, God is bigger than that, and if you're going through a family crisis God is bigger than that. Racism and hatred are becoming a greater issue than ever before. Guess what? God is bigger than that.

(Philippians 4:19 KJV) says "But my God shall supply all your need according to his riches in glory by Christ Jesus." God has not forgotten about you, God will never leave you or forsake you, he doesn't sleep, he's always watching over you even when you don't know. So, I say, whatever is hurting you God is bigger than that, he will supply all our needs. He will always reign over all things.

After my journey with addiction and joining the Army. I worked hard on my sobriety and my military career, and I got through days, nights, months, and years. Before I retired in 2009 with 21 years in the Army, I went back to school and received my Associate's, Bachelor's, and Master's degrees. I delivered my trial sermon and received a Minister's License in 2004 and have been preaching since. I also decided to become a published author publishing my first book during the COVID-19 pandemic. If I can emerge positively, not turning left or right and journey forwarded so can you. With God, you can control your Destiny by walking boldly in a new direction. God is bigger than your dilemmas.

Have faith by placing your trust in God, instead of in people or circumstances. Be prepared to take whatever steps God directs you to take into your future. Although you can't be sure what life will create, you can be certain of God's promise that he will be with you, lead, guide, and direct you through your troubles. Keep a positive spiritual attitude with your head up and eyes on God. We all make mistakes. None of us ARE PERFECT. It's how we learn, and if we are willing to admit we made wrong choices, we grow in wisdom.

God is magnified, that is what that word bigger means. He becomes larger than anything that you are confronting right now. It does not matter where it derived from, or how long it has remained,

God is bigger than that!

If you would just believe all the ministering angels in heaven surrounding, you to bring your issues to pass. We are conquering therefore our troubles shall come to pass sooner than we think because God is:

Bigger than your past
Bigger than your pain
Bigger than your anger
Bigger than your fear
Bigger than your scar
Bigger than your insecurities
Bigger than your sin.

When things don't happen on our timetable, it can be tempting to get discouraged. But in the season of waiting, that's when you must dig your heels in and refuse to give up! You must know that God is doing something in you at the same time, he is doing something for you. I want to remind you that facing a difficult time right now or in the future, but beyond that difficulty is a new level of God's favor. That challenge is not there to stop you it is there to develop you.

Don't stop Chapter 19 awaits!!!!

Chapter 19

God Said, "Not Yet"

For weeks you have prayed and begged for answers to your questions that afflict your days. You think the journey you are on is working out for you. You even begin to plan your victory dance to success. Then God laid an obstacle in the road, and you end up at a standstill. It brings you to no options at present. You've studied God's word, attend church, and do all the right things as a result, you feel cheated and beat down and asking God why you couldn't have or receive want he promised. You want to receive your blessing right now because it would be the right time for you. You willingly accept what God has for you.

"For my thoughts are not your thoughts, and your ways are not MY WAYS." (Isaiah 55:8 KJV)

Have you ever asked the question when Lord? When will my blessing come? I put things aside to do the things that God has called me to do after the door has been shut. It is just a matter of the right time for God to release the NOT YET to THE TIME IS NOW!!!!

God does answer prayers, bring your concerns to him. He promises to hear you as you come to him. Sometimes, our prayers may seem to go unanswered because God is keeping us from something that isn't best for us. He may answer prayer with "Yes," "No" or "Not Yet" That might not be what we want to hear. We cannot see what God can see because we are eager. Our troubles impede our prayers, and we must take care of that first. That trouble is sin.

I can remember turning 21 years old. I bought a car and decided to go out and celebrate. One night I drove to a birthday party in a high-rise apartment 30 miles from where I lived at my parent's home. This party had a lot of free alcohol and drugs that seemed to be what I thought I needed to have a good time. I recall drinking and drinking and partying what happen next was a blur. All I could remember was getting into my car and driving on the highway, then I woke up in the driveway of my parent's home, scary? Yes! What I did not realize at that time, God said, "Not Yet, it is not your time." I have covered you again regardless of how reckless and irresponsible you are. Why? Because I have work for you to do someday.

For years after that incident, after turning my life over to God, I felt strong about my calling which requires writing and ministering to other men. It started with jabs to my heart. Then those jabs turned into more regular pings. Therefore, I received validation to start writing. And God revealed to me in so many ways the need for encouraging words to go out to people who may be hurting. I kept seeing this need to take all the brokenness and messy stuff and turn it into praise. I saw that men and women needed a word of inspiration and support more than ever. So, I began to write expressing what I thought would be enough to satisfy what my heart was hearing from God.

When you apply for a credit card, a loan for a car or house and do not get approve, that maybe a blessing with the HELP from God ...."NOT YET". We cannot see what is ahead of us. God can see if we can afford a credit card, car of House therefore at that time the answer is "Not Yet".

As always wanting something different for my life is my hope. With this hope I discovered more about my calling and purpose. Those jabs to my heart begin to beat even louder. To be honest, sometimes I still did not know what my calling is going to look like throughout this race, but I can tell you this, I feel exceptionally good about writing, which is a significant part of my calling.

I imagined myself writing books and having my words bounce off a page and onto someone's heart. With God's blessings, I use my words to let you know that you are not alone. There is someone out there that understands. I would start to write and lose concentration. "It just wasn't my time" So, when the answer is "Not Yet" he is preparing you for greater, and spiritual maturity that will be the vital piece to understanding our calling.

The final Chapter is next

Chapter 20

Spiritual Encouragement

You're pacing the floor day and night wondering how to solve a situation that seems to be out of your hands. You find yourself supposedly in a conversation with someone but in a daze because your mind is on your problems. You are on your job behind in your work but cannot concentrate due to your troubles. Family crisis, financial burdens, relationship difficulties, or struggles with your leadership at work. God says be still and know I am God. I am already at work; it is already done. Sometimes we must encourage ourselves when there isn't anyone available to encourage us.

Too often I used to think that I was the only one in control of my life. God helped me to see that he is in control. We can blame others for our mishaps, situations, and issues but at the end of the day, it is faith that leads to handling our problems and always with the help of the Lord.

Sometimes in life, we need some encouragement, the best support is spiritual encouragement, so I pray that God reassures your heart today. Know that you are loved, and God is near. Just hang in there during these difficult times. God knows what you are going through, and you can know that He is working even as we sleep. Be encouraged !

The Lord is always near, and you are never alone. Even when times are hard, and our days seem dark, God can shine his light into our lives and give us great peace. You will be filled with the hope of God's love, joy, and peace. If you should ever feel alone or afraid, know that God is nearer than you think. I pray that you will feel the presence of God and that you will draw strength and hope as you trust Him to be your comfort and your faith will see you through.

Encouraging words can help you think straight, bounce back, and move forward towards a normal life. They are not just for you to consider, but for you to apply as well whenever someone is in need. Spiritual words work for everyone anytime, anywhere. If you are going through something, or at a fork in the road and it is too much for you to bear, be still and seek God's help. The best solution would be fasting and praying. Be encouraged!

One day we can be standing on top of the world and the next day we can be hit with major problems that we do not know how to handle. As we experience life's ups and downs it will be like being on a roller coaster ride. Just like the Roller Coaster Ride, before we reach the joy of success at the top, we will be targeted in life plunge downward. We are faced with fears, unsettling feelings, and skepticism of the risk we are taking with us on the ride.

Words of Encouragement:

"Don't be afraid, for I am with you. Don't be discouraged, for I am your God. I will strengthen you and help you. I will hold you up with my victorious right hand." (Isaiah 41:10 KIV)

"Therefore, do not worry about tomorrow, for tomorrow will worry about itself. Each day has enough trouble of its own."– (Matthew 6:34 NIV)

"He gives strength to the weary and increases the power of the weak." (Isaiah 40:29 KIV)

"For the Spirit God gave us does not make us timid, but gives us power, love and self-discipline." (2 Timothy 1:7 KIV)

True peace does not come because of eliminating burdens and failures. It comes because of one thing, and that is an intimate relationship with the Lord Jesus Christ. He is where fear ends, and peace begins.

When we let ourselves submit to our doubts, we are letting doubts take away our impending success. If we want to achieve success, we must face our fears and problems. Unless we do, we will be forever wedged into our disasters so be strong and courageous trust in the Lord. Do not be discouraged, for the LORD your God will be with you wherever you go.

I pray that you receive great value from these words of encouragement. Perhaps they will guide you on the path to your Christian journey.

A Note to the Readers

Thank you for joining me on this project. I hope this book touched your soul the same way it has touched mine.

If you enjoyed this book and my previous book "In the Midnight Hour" and you have a minute to spare, I would appreciate a short review on the websites below . Your help in spreading the word is greatly appreciated. Reviews from readers like you make a huge difference in helping new readers find books like "Embracing Strength & Purpose In the Midst of Your Storm". The sites are as follows:

*amazon.com:
*barnesandnoble.com:
*Westbow.com

Thank you! God Bless!
Rev. Michael Gamble

P.S. If you'd like to receive occasional updates you can send me an email at michaelgamble821@outlook.com …. Thank you!

Printed in the United States
by Baker & Taylor Publisher Services